Please return / renew by date shown.
You can renew it at:
norlink.norfolk.gov.uk
or by telephone: 0344 800 8006
Please have your library card & PIN ready

NORFOLK LIBRARY
AND INFORMATION SERVICE

History Makers

Guy Fawkes
and the Gunpowder Plot

Sarah Ridley

W
FRANKLIN WATTS
LONDON•SYDNEY

First published in 2009 by
Franklin Watts
338 Euston Road
London NW1 3BH

Franklin Watts Australia
Hachette Children's Books
Level 17/207 Kent Street
Sydney NSW 2000

ISBN 978 0 7496 8712 0

Dewey classification: 940.53

Series editor: Jeremy Smith
Art director: Jonathan Hair
Design: Simon Morse
Cover design: Jonathan Hair
Picture research: Sarah Ridley

Picture credits: Mary Evans Picture Library:
16, 17, 18, 19, 20. Robert Harding/Getty
Images: 6, 21. Andrew Holt/Getty Images: 4.
Hulton Archive/Getty Images: front cover l,
9, 13, 22. Index/Bridgeman Art Library: 12.
Gideon Mendell/Corbis: 23. NMM
London/Bridgeman Art Library: 14. NPG
London/Bridgeman Art Library: 5.
Picturepoint/Topham: 15. El Prado
Madrid/Bridgeman Art Library: 8.
Private Collection/Getty Images: 10.
Roger-Viollet/Getty Images: 7. SCP/BAL: 11.
Stapleton/HIP/Topfoto; front cover r, 1.

Franklin Watts is a division of Hachette
Children's Books, an Hachette Livre UK
company.

www.hachettelivre.co.uk

Printed in China

Remember, remember
The fifth of November:
Gunpowder, treason and plot.
I see no reason
Why gunpowder-treason
Should ever be forgot.
Anon

Contents

Early life   4

School   6

Adventure   8

A new king   10

Spanish help   12

The plot   14

Tunnel and cellar   16

The secret letter   18

Torture   20

Death sentence   22

Glossary/Index   24

Early life

Guy Fawkes was born in the city of York in 1570. His father was a lawyer and the family followed the Protestant form of Christianity.

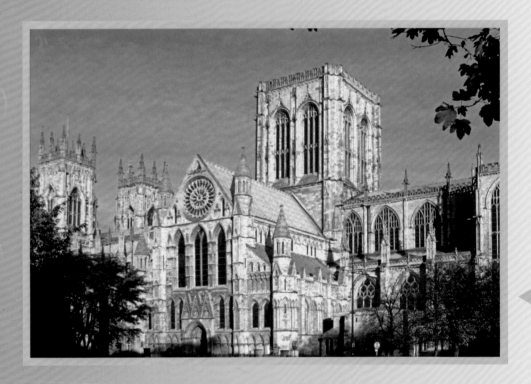

Guy lived close to York Minster.

1558 ▶

Elizabeth I becomes queen.

▲ This portrait shows Elizabeth I in her coronation clothes.

Queen Elizabeth I ruled England at this time. She was a Protestant, as were many of her people. Others were Catholics, a form of Christianity that was illegal at the time.

1566 ▶

Mary Queen of Scots has a baby boy, James. He will become King James I of England.

1570 ▶

Guy Fawkes is born.

School

When he was five, Guy went to St Peter's School in York. There the headmaster worshipped secretly as a Catholic. Guy became a Catholic as well.

▲ Guy walked to school. He lived on this street, which still survives.

1575 ▶

Guy goes to school.

1578 ▶

Guy's father dies.

Catholics and Protestants had different ways of worship. In England, Catholics were not allowed to hold mass, their religious service.

If Catholic priests were caught saying mass, they could be hung.

1580 ▶

Francis Drake returns from sailing around the world.

Adventure

After school, Guy wanted adventure. He decided to become a paid soldier for the Spanish king, Philip II (right), who was a Catholic. Guy became an expert with gunpowder.

1587 ▶

Elizabeth I orders the execution of Mary Queen of Scots, a Catholic.

1588 ▶

Guy leaves school.

▲ A drawing of Guy. He was tall with red hair.

1588 ▶

The English defeat the Spanish Armada.

1589 ▶

Guy becomes a soldier.

A new king

This portrait of Elizabeth I was painted towards the end of her life, although the artist made her look young.

Back in England, Elizabeth I was growing old. During her life, there were several plots to replace her with a Catholic ruler.

March

1603 ▶

Elizabeth I dies.

James I of England and VI of Scotland.

When Elizabeth I died, James VI of Scotland became the new king of England. Catholics hoped that life would improve for them.

April

1603 ▶

James VI of Scotland is crowned James I of England.

Spanish help

Some English Catholics hoped that Spain would help them replace James I with a Catholic ruler. Guy even visited the Spanish king, Philip III, to ask for help.

▶ Philip III of Spain wanted peace, not war, with James I.

1603 ▶

Guy visits Philip III in Spain, who is not interested in plotting against James 1.

Guy left Spain, disappointed. He went back to being a soldier and soon met another soldier called Thomas Winter.

Thomas Winter was a soldier and a Catholic.

January
1604

James I says that Catholics will not be allowed to worship freely.

February
1604

Robert Catesby, John Wright and Thomas Wintour begin the Gunpowder Plot.

13

The plot

The plotters meet and plan to blow up James I.

Thomas Winter introduced Guy to his cousin, Robert Catesby. Catesby had a daring plan to blow up James I and Parliament. The plotters would replace James with his daughter, Princess Elizabeth.

◄ A portrait of Princess Elizabeth. She was only nine years old at the time of the plot

May
1604 ▶

14

Wintour is sent to Flanders to recruit Guy Fawkes.

The plotters met at a London inn called the Duck and Drake.

CONCILIVM SEPTEM NOBILIVM ANGLORVM CONIVRANTIVM IN NECEM IACOBI · I ·
MAGNÆ BRITANNIÆ REGIS TOTIVSQ · ANGLICI CONVOCATI PARLEMENTI

Robert Winter
Bates
Christopher Wright
Iohn Wright
Thomas Percy
Guido Fawkes
Robert Catesby
Thomas Winter

The Gunpowder Plot conspirators (left to right): Bates, Robert Winter, Christopher Wright, John Wright, Thomas Percy, Guy Fawkes, Robert Catesby, and Thomas Winter.

May
1604 ▶

The plotters rent a house close to Westminster Hall.

15

Tunnel and cellar

The plotters rented a house close to Westminster Hall, where Parliament met. They tried to dig a tunnel under the hall but it was too difficult.

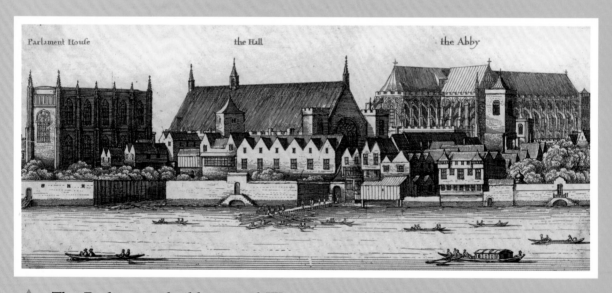

▲ The Parliament buildings and Westminster Abbey in the 1600s.

May 1604 ▶
The plotters start to dig a tunnel.

July 1604 ▶
Great Plague returns to London, delaying the plot.

Guy and another plotter moved barrels of gunpowder by boat.

By luck, the plotters heard about an empty cellar right underneath Westminster Hall. They rented it and filled it with barrels of gunpowder.

March

1605 ▶

The plotters stop digging a tunnel and rent a cellar instead.

May

1605 ▶

The plotters place barrels of gunpowder in the cellar.

17

The secret letter

All was set for the explosion to take place on 5 November 1605, the day when King James would be in Parliament. Then, at the end of October, a Catholic called Lord Monteagle received a letter warning him to stay away from Parliament.

FAC-SIMILE OF THE LETTER WRITTEN TO LORD MONTEAGLE
WHICH LED TO THE DISCOVERY OF THE GUNPOWDER PLOT.

This is the letter that Lord Monteagle received.

October
1605

Lord Monteagle receives a secret letter.

Lord Monteagle told the King's advisors and, slowly, they took action. On 4 November soldiers searched Westminster Hall. Down in the cellar they found Guy Fawkes.

 Guy guarding the gunpowder. This illustration imagines him laying the fuse to set off the explosion.

4 November
1605 ▶

The plot is discovered.

Torture

Guy was arrested. In order to give the other plotters a chance to escape, Guy kept quiet. After several days of torture, he spoke about the plot.

▲ Guy was stretched on the rack, a form of torture shown here.

5 November
1605 ▶

Londoners light bonfires to celebrate that their king survived the plot.

7th November
1605 ▶

After days of torture, Guy Fawkes starts to give details of the plot.

 The surviving plotters were put in the Tower of London.

The rest of the plotters fled and hid. A few days later they were surrounded by 200 soldiers. After a dramatic shoot-out killed four of them, the rest were arrested.

8th November
1605 ▶

Soldiers discover the plotters' hiding place. Four are shot dead, the rest are arrested.

Death sentence

At the Gunpowder Plot trial, the plotters were found guilty of treason. This meant death. One by one, they were executed.

This drawing shows the execution of the plotters.

January
1606

Gunpowder Trial. The plotters are sentenced to death.

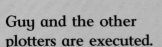 A modern bonfire night party.

British people still remember the Gunpowder Plot and how close it came to killing James I. On 5 November they light bonfires, burn a 'guy' and set off fireworks.

November
1606 ▶

Guy and the other
plotters are executed.

Glossary

Catholic A member of the Roman Catholic Church.

Cellar An underground room.

Gunpowder An explosive powder.

Parliament The group of people which makes the laws of a country, and the place where they meet.

Protestant A member of any Christian church that separated from the Roman Catholic Church in the 16th century.

Spanish Armada A fleet of ships sent by Philip II of Spain to invade England.

Treason A crime against the king or the country.

Trial When evidence is looked at in a court, to decide whether someone is guilty or not.

Index

Catesby, Robert 14
Catholics 5, 6, 7, 8, 10, 11, 12, 13, 18, 24
childhood 4, 5, 6

Elizabeth I 4, 5, 8, 10, 11
execution of plotters 22, 23

gunpowder 8, 17, 19, 24
Gunpowder Plot 14-20, 22, 23

James I 5, 11, 12, 13, 14, 18, 19, 20, 23

Lord Monteagle 18, 19

Parliament 14, 16, 18, 24
Philip II/III 8, 12, 24
plotters, the 14, 15, 16, 17, 20, 21, 22, 23
Princess Elizabeth 14
Protestants 4, 5, 7, 24

soldiers 8, 9, 13, 19, 21
Spain 8, 9, 12, 13, 24

treason 22, 24
trial 22, 24

Winter, Thomas 13, 14